the flesh is not a prison

by Graham Cwinn

"If our life lacks brimstone, i.e., a constant magic, it is because we choose to observe our acts and lose ourselves in considerations of their imagined form instead of being impelled by their force."
— Antonin Artaud

"What differentiates us from the pagans is that, at the root of all their beliefs, there is a dreadful effort not to believe in man, in order to maintain contact with the whole of creation, with divinity, that is."
— Antonin Artaud

"Again, we are the planet, we are the universe, all is contained in all. The mystics of all traditions agree that this is the core wisdom of the world."
— Gast Bouschet

"This is a time to tear off our human skin. This is a time to become powerful without being dominant. This is a time to reimagine our place in the world. The world has become too human, "all too human.""
— Gast Bouschet

"Posthumanist philosophy constitutes the human as: (a) physically, chemically, and biologically enmeshed and dependent on the environment; (b) moved to action through interactions that generate affects, habits, and reason; and (c) possessing no attribute that is uniquely human but is instead made up of a larger evolving ecosystem."
— Diane Marie Keeling and Marguerite Nguyen Lehman

I.

the flesh is not a prison

you are not your anguish,
or the sum of your experiences.

yes, they happened:
they happened to you.

you might relive them every day.

yet in spite of it all
you are simply yourself.

and it is beautiful.

the world is failing us

I see you, broken and dejected,
seeking treatment and finding none.

there is the desire to lash out,
to push people away from us.

but

we must cling to each other
lift each other up
provide the healing that society
has deprived us of.

mutation

break apart if you need to.
take the time to breathe in
the pain. let it be yours.

and then reassemble.
grow around it.

become something more.

untying the noose

not a day goes by where I
don't think about killing myself.

my mind replays images
of my body hanging from
the bridge near my house.

then I think about who would find
me: they would be scarred forever.

and what about the people I leave
behind? devastated beyond repair.

what if I fail?

what then?

I will live with the shame of yet
another failed suicide attempt.

attempt number six.

I can't do that to them.
I can't do that to myself.

I am in terrible pain.
I am alive.

liberation

for decades I felt I was trapped inside myself.

I realize now there is a whole world in me,
and that it resonates with the world around me.

I am free to wander the caverns of my skull;
to swim in my veins; to dance inside my limbs.

and I realize that the more I dance,
the more others want to dance with me.

my brain

it is not normal.
it is riddled with
illness.

it is also filled with
a desire to be at
peace with itself.

it is the only one
I will ever have

and I am learning
to love it.

unearthing a fossil

encased in darkness.
for eons it is all you
have ever known.

but now the light is seeping in.
it scrapes away the earth.
it carves a space, a space
which it also craves.

it releases you from your
shell of a former existence.

that is all behind you.
it is time to open your
eyes and experience

life.

flailing, not failing

your broken teeth
are not a failure.

the mountain of dishes
is not a failure.

the unanswered messages
you keep meaning to reply
to are not a failure.

your detachment from
work is not a failure.

forgetting to take your
meds is not a failure.

give credit to your suffering.
acknowledge you are surviving.

dum spiro spero
(while I breathe, I hope)

inhale.
exhale.

find the strength to
return to yourself.

mantra

I will

hypnotize you
and make you

believe you are
worthy of love

from yourself
and others.

death is not the end.

one day we will relinquish
our final, rattling breath.

disassemble.

energy and matter
change into
something new.

all our agonies and
grief are put to rest.

remember that we
are a part of reality

and we shall see all of it
and bask in its glory
forever.

"we're building trainwrecks in the setting sun"

Detroit. 1956. autoworkers; drive-in movies; start-up business talks about
Motown jazz; neon lights and all the dazzling promises of freedom. the Dream.
but beneath all those fur coats and Neo-bourgeoisie suits and hats and canes
there was still an aching sensation: they were reaching for something that isn't
there, their minds never knowing what exactly to cling to, and all that blind grasp-
ing and gasping on expensive white lines

[or maybe staggering in defeat along a yellow dotted line, pants at the ankles and
policemen in navy-blue shaking their heads in what they mask as humour but,
deep down, is shame: they have seen this depravity in everyone, in themselves,
and they cover it all up with a laugh and a night in the drunk tank]

just to forget that they had given up on finding intrinsic value decades ago.

or maybe from the day they were born, the moment they were squelched into this
world sticky with placenta and shrieking for not just nutrition and shelter, but love,
they knew that it was going to be hopeless...

with eyes already grown, but head still too small, I gazed about the interior of
the car in youthful bewilderment; starting occasionally at the harsh barks and
screeches coming from the larger ME's in the driver and passenger seats.

unable to understand, and not wanting to [I could think only of vague and seem-
ingly contradictory notions such as "The Obligations Of A Happy Family," and,
"The Right To Suffer"], I shifted my attention to the floor mat: it smelled of fresh
rubber, but it already had been caked with mud and dust and crumbs and hair
and all the nitty-gritty nasty little things that we like to deny are there; and when
these accumulate to the point of public observation, the mat is tossed away in a
disgraceful rejection that only lasts until a new one is purchased from the store
and put in its stead -- it had already been forgotten the moment it was replaced
-- and this new, better floor mat was to suffer the same fate.

I had been birthed into a brave, new world; a shining hope in dark, uncertain
times. I am not referring solely to wars of the political spectrum, but of those
which fester in the private sector because it is believed that here, only, can they
be carved out of the flesh in secret, like a tumor [as if a cure for all the victim's
nameless ailments]; unaware, or stubbornly refusing to admit, that such a
confinement led consistently, unfailingly, into grimmer places. in a post-Enlight-
enment world, we are still strapped to the rusted rails of an archaic Determinism:
hurtling towards a trainwreck repeating itself over and over and over and over
and over and over in a real[reel]- time nightmare until someone says, "wait. stop.
it doesn't have to be this way."

and though I was a mere toddler and didn't process any of these disturbing truths
via my still- undeveloped frontal lobe, they conversed and schemed in hushed
and deadly tones that coursed through my veins; flooded my ears with the
rushing of a vast ocean, helplessly

spilling into the dull, whirring vacuum of space.

II.

art is life is art is life...

art does not imitate life.
life does not imitate art.

they are one and the same,
locked in a ritual dance

of triumph and mourning.

a sense of purpose

a culmination of our life experiences
has distorted us, forced us into
hideous contortions that separate
us from ourselves and the world.

we learn to live in a false reality
where the only thing we know is pain.

but there is more to life.

I want to create something
that will shatter that reality
and bring us back to this one.

I want to help us return to ourselves.

Ouroboros

I see it every day:

humans eating each other.

when the cannibalism
makes them sick, they
point fingers anywhere
but at themselves.

they eat the world,
not realizing it is a part
of them.

and when there is nothing left,
no flesh or trees to devour,
what then?

I wish to make humans vomit
up all that they have consumed

and maybe they will love
what is splayed before them.

"sleep is an illusion in which we continue to live."

I had a dream
that my friend
from the hospital

was no longer confined
to that ghastly ward;

that he could walk
at last, not bound
to a wheelchair.

I wonder where he is now
and if he has conquered
his nightmares.

"we all go home or nobody goes home."

leave none behind.
every living thing
has inherent value.

by abandoning the downtrodden,
letting them slip through the cracks,

we are losing a part of ourselves.

"I saw what you did and how much it hurt you."

the ones who harmed
you were also bleeding.

and now you bleed on others.
and they bleed on even more
people in a vicious swirl.

I pray that you will see
the pattern of violence
you are perpetuating

and that you break
the cycle of torment.

vampires

they feed on others relentlessly.
sucking life from necks that are
already tired from the weight
of troubled minds.

garlic and crosses will
not drive them away.

we must teach them
to be human again.

new skin

I used to be bitter.
I took my anger
out on others.

some of them
will never forgive
me.

they don't have
to and I don't
blame them.

the integral factor
was realizing that
I had to change.

revolution of being

each step leads
me farther away
from what I was

and closer to
who I truly am.

exaltation

lost for years
in a multiplicity
of forms,

now I realize
there has always
only been one self:

me.

a universe
of microbes

living in harmony.

III.

**"but what can you do if the body is weak
and the mind is too sick?"**

capitalism informs me I must work to be
human, while I barely scrape by on disability.

this isn't enough to live.

but I don't have the strength to give myself
back to the system, back to the machine.

teetering on the edge of homelessness
and starvation. how can I enjoy life
when I fear the worst will come crashing

down?

screams and survival

will you assess me and deem me suitable for treatment?
or will you claim my disorder is complicated and turn me away?

there is an urgency which you do not seem
to understand. each day may very well be
my last, each day I am on the brink
of oblivion.

am I not worthy of being saved?

the cult of psychiatry

they place a template
on your being in order
to determine how you
are sick.

despite relying on personal
accounts, there is little
regard to your input.

what matters is that they save
a very specific subset of patients

*(look at how many people
we are helping!!!!!!!!!!!!!!!)*

and if you don't meet their criteria,

you will be left to die.

persistence of the spirit

it lives in my flesh.

at times my illness diminishes it
(for the mind is also in the flesh)

yet it is impossible to vanquish.

demonology

hallucinations.
delusions.
mania.
depression.

my enemies adorn themselves
in many disguises; introduce
themselves with false names.

but I am slowly, secretly, learning
their true names. and I will have

power over them.

Ward

scrawling sigils
in corners

to protect you
from doctors
nurses
patients
spirits.

scrawling sigils
on your hands

to purify the self

as if to say,

"my hands are safe.
you can trust them."

"fire, gesture, blood, cry"

with wild gesticulation
I shall explain the passion
which burns throughout
my being.

a passion to fucking rip
the veil of this false
reality away, and reveal
to everyone their naked
and true selves.

only then will the world
be able to move forward.

I truly believe this.

unity

I refuse to believe in a separation
of body, mind, and soul.

they comingle in an ecstacic ritual of being.

but when society cares not for the mind,
or the soul, but the body, only...

this condemns us all to a slow,
torturous, living death from which

there is only one escape.

"the weapons of my breath"

a man once said of me:

"I'll be impressed if this guy
still has a voice by the time
he's 35."

that was eight years ago.
I am 34 now and my scream

is more terrifying than ever.

"we are here for you."

"let us condemn the sick for demanding better care."

"let us raise prices and bring people to
desperation, while boasting record profits."

"let us frown upon any person who takes
allotted sick days, if they even have any."

"let us raise the cost of housing, forcing more
people onto the streets and into group homes
that, let's face it, are horrid at best."

"let us now wave the flag of compassion,
a virtue signal to hide all our evil deeds."

it boils my blood,
causes me to cry out
in abject frustration

when faced with the cruelty
of systems and institutions.

wait list

18 months.

this is how long it will have taken
to finally speak with a specialist

about my chronic suicidality.

there is no guarantee of treatment,
first they must decide if I fit into
their neat little boxes.

they must deliberate over whether my
schizoaffective depression is worth it.

if not I must return to the hospital,
decay in that awful ward, wait for
an eternity.

my intimate history with medications

fluoxetine
desvenlafaxine
trazodone
lithium
ziprasidone
mirtazapine
haloperidol
lamotrigine
olanzapine
paliperidone
bupropion
quetiapine
escitalopram
duloxetine
aripiprazole
prazosin
pregabalin

"buried by time and dust"

the most powerful thing in this universe
is the sweeping, unifying force of love.

and yet it is the easiest power
for us to forget how to use.

we are afraid of loving ourselves
because we see it as egotism.

we are afraid of loving each other
because we confuse compassion
with weakness, and most of all

with communism, which has
nothing to do with tyranny.

we fear each other,
we fear ourselves,

and love is buried by time and dust.

IV.

first breath / intent

Saturn hovers above
our heads; enters the body;
feeds the flame in which

His teeth did brightly shine.

when things conspire together

energy and matter
can not be created
or destroyed; only
transformed.

we are all part of a grand system
that is perpetually and tirelessly
ebbing and flowing amongst
different phases of being
and non-being.

even the space between atoms
is an integral facet of existence.

our bodies, composed of trillions
of microbial beings, operate
in unison: a miraculous yet real
example of what can happen

when things conspire together.

"we worship thee"

we worship thee. we worship thee. we worship thee.
we worship thee. we worship thee. we worship thee.
we worship thee. we worship thee. we worship thee.
we worship thee. we worship thee. we worship thee.
we worship thee. we worship thee. we worship thee.
a light. we worship thee. we worship thee. we worship thee.
a presence. we worship thee. we worship thee. we worship thee.
a voice. we worship thee. we worship thee. we worship thee.
we worship thee. we worship thee. we worship thee.
we worship thee. we worship thee. we worship thee.
we worship thee. we worship thee. we worship thee.
we worship thee. we worship thee. we worship thee.
we worship thee. we worship thee. we worship thee.

"the Earth wants us dead"

the Earth wants us dead.

I taste it in the sap of trees.
enraged, bitter, foul.

the Earth wants us dead.

can you smell it in the air?
cloying, suffocating, a miasma.

the Earth wants us dead.

tectonic shifts proclaim
the approach of our doom.

the Earth wants us dead.

a warning that we must
change our ways, or it

will be the end of everything.

a metaphysics of suffering

a grey squirrel was hit by a car yesterday.

I didn't see it happen but its carcass
lay flattened on the road. a crow
from my tree began to feed.

I watched the entire process: the flaying
and consuming of skin, tendon, flesh.
organs pulled out from ravenous perforations.

the crow, satisfied with its meal,
took flight into the clear blue sky.

last night it gently rained and
now even the bones are gone.

post-human

we must cease imagining
ourselves as apex beings
worthy of owning the planet.

this is destroying us all.

instead, we must conceive
of humans as pieces of a
vast network, where each
living and non-living thing
is worshipped, together.

humility and respect:
this is what the earth
is asking of us.

escape

your limbic system
controls you.

I see it informing
every decision
you make.

it's not your fault.

when we are damaged by traumatic experiences
our brain becomes disconnected and we no longer
process information via the frontal lobe.

to tell someone who is having a flashback
to "snap out of it, you're acting irrationally"

is to condemn them for the suffering
they have already endured, silently:
that gaping blackness that devours

everything.

yet I know that, with time
and practice and a healthy
support system, you will
finally reconnect the lost
regions of your brain.

I know you can escape.

a return to sorcery

this is a demand that we, as a society,
return to the mystical aspect of being.

by mystical, I mean the recognition
that there is a grand energy in all
things, and the wonder and reverence
instilled by this recognition.

too many of us feel aimless and lost.

whether one is religious or not,
it is essential to feel like one is
a part of something greater
than ourselves. we did not
evolve to be solitary creatures.

we crave connection and acceptance.
what better way to discover that
than by opening up to the universe?

we must once again ritualize
the aspects of existence
that connect us to ourselves
and everything that surrounds
us.

masquerade of being

remove your costume
of preconceived notions
and reveal your true
self.

remove the lenses which
distort your perception
and see the world as it
truly is.

mourning

I am grieving
for all the futures
I have lost
to trauma.

I am mourning
for my past self
and all the times
I was hurt.

trying desperately to
create a new present
and future for myself.

the war against suicide

I have realized that these thoughts of suicide
are not representative of how I feel about my life.

they simply exist.

and I must combat them with fire and steel;
words and worship; creation and integration;
all the tools and weapons at my disposal
shall be used in this war against the urge
to kill myself.

Light Bearer

when the light shone upon me
I felt a powerful presence within
my being. a voice uttered a mingling
of warnings and praise. I was shown
two paths: for years I wandered down
the wrong one. now, however, I have been
offered another opportunity to change.

I see you in everything — I see everything in you

I breathe you in.

I sense you in the air.
the trees. the earth.
the animals and insects.

I feel you in the rays of the sun.
you wash over me as drops of rain.

projection of the True body

behold.

through this cruel dance I have transformed.
now I walk, with an aura of flame, amongst
others who limp, stagger, fight —
yes, truly fight — we fight for our very lives.

I have become
a being-within-being:

mind, soul, and flesh rejoice
in harmony with the earth.

acknowledgments

"we're building trainwrecks in the setting sun" is a lyric by Thee Silver Mt Zion

"sleep is an illusion in which we continue to live." is a quote by Antonin Artaud

"we all go home or nobody goes home" is a quote from G.I. Joe: The Animated Movie

"I saw what you did and how much it hurt you" is a lyric by The Haunting

"fire, gesture, blood, cry" is a quote by Antonin Artaud

"the weapons of my breath" is a quote by Antonin Artaud

"Buried By Time And Dust" is a song by Mayhem

"His teeth did brightly shine" is a song by Earth

"We worship thee" is a lyric by Abigor

"The Earth Wants Us Dead" is an album by Sea of Bones

"Projection of the True Body" is a drawing by Antonin Artaud

cover art by Graham Cwinn
formatting by Max Southwood
author photo by Shannon Duncan (Level Up Photography)

special thanks: Max, Liam, Savannah, Julien, Rosie, Reed, Brendan, Blake, Sara Y., Jake, Kyle, Sara H., Evan, Dave, Shawn, John, my family, and everyone else who has supported me during my darkest and brightest days.

ISBN: 978-1-9991444-9-4

thingsinmychest.bigcartel.com

about the author

Graham Cwinn is an author, musician, and artist living in Ottawa, Ontario. He has self- published several poetry collections, and is writing and illustrating a graphic novel. His poems have appeared twice in *In/Words Magazine*. Graham also runs the small press Things in my Chest. His work offers glimmers of hope in the face of schizoaffective disorder, trauma, and loss.

www.ingramcontent.com/pod-product-compliance
Lightning Source LLC
Chambersburg PA
CBHW031236120626
46545CB00003B/1141